EVERYDAY S T E M

HOW THE CLOUD WORKS

ANNE MARIE FORD

Cavendish
Square
New York

Published in 2019 by Cavendish Square Publishing, LLC
243 5th Avenue, Suite 136, New York, NY 10016

Website: cavendishsq.com

This publication represents the opinions and views of the author based on his or her personal experience, knowledge, and research. The information in this book serves as a general guide only. The author and publisher have used their best efforts in preparing this book and disclaim liability rising directly or indirectly from the use and application of this book.

All websites were available and accurate when this book was sent to press.

Library of Congress Cataloging-in-Publication Data

Names: Ford, Jeanne Marie, 1971- author.
Title: How the cloud works / Jeanne Marie Ford.
Description: First edition. | New York : Cavendish Square, 2019. |
Series: Everyday STEM | Includes bibliographical references and index. |
Audience: 2-5.
Identifiers: LCCN 2017048050 (print) | LCCN 2017059295 (ebook) |
ISBN 9781502637437 (ebook) | ISBN 9781502637406 (library bound) |
ISBN 9781502637413 (pbk.) | ISBN 9781502637420 (6 pack)
Subjects: LCSH: Cloud computing--Juvenile literature. |
Computer networks--Juvenile literature.
Classification: LCC QA76.585 (ebook) | LCC QA76.585 .F665 2019 (print) |
DDC 004.67/82--dc23
LC record available at https://lccn.loc.gov/2017048050

Editorial Director: David McNamara
Editor: Fletcher Doyle/Meghan Lamb
Copy Editor: Nathan Heidelberger
Associate Art Director: Amy Greenan
Designer: Christina Shults
Production Coordinator: Karol Szymczuk
Photo Research: J8 Media

The photographs in this book are used by permission and through the courtesy of:
Cover, Dotshock/Shutterstock.com; p. 4 Pakhnyushchy/Shutterstock.com; p. 6 justyle/Shutterstock.com; p. 7 Tom Kelley Archive/Retrofile/Getty Images; p. 8 Science & Society Picture Library/Getty Images; p. 9 Sagel & Kranefeld/Corbis/Getty Images; p. 10 Philip Preston/The Boston Globe/Getty Images; p. 12 Mrklong/Shutterstock.com; p. 13 fad82/Shutterstock.com; p. 14 lOvE lOvE/Shutterstock.com; p. 15 Pictafolio/istockphoto.com; p. 16 backtasan/Shutterstock.com; p.19 Nicholas Free/istockphoto.com; p. 20 Rawpixel.com/Shutterstock.com; p. 21 Izabela Habur/iStockphoto.com; p. 23 arka38/Shutterstock.com; p. 24 ESB Professional/Shutterstock.com; p. 25 Paisit Teeraphatsakool/Shutterstock.com; p. 26 Carolina K. Smith MD/Shutterstock.com.

Printed in the United States of America

CONTENTS

Clouds in the sky are made of water droplets.

CHAPTER 1
WHAT IS THE CLOUD?

Clouds are formed by the collection of millions of tiny water droplets. "Cloud computing" refers to millions of **bytes** of **data** collected on the internet. The cloud is a type of storage. It allows people to share and access data online.

Information saved on a device is called **local** storage. Hard drives and memory cards are types of local storage. They can hold limited

amounts of data.
Cloud servers also
save information.
However, they
have much larger
memories. They
allow users to store
far more data online.

Microchips store data on
memory cards.

Today's computers, smartphones, and tablets
use cloud technology. Many **apps** are cloud-
based. Messenger is one popular cloud-based

FAST FACT

According to a 2016 report from CompTIA, 90 percent of
businesses surveyed use some type of cloud technology.

The first computers were mainframes shared by many users.

app. Most people access the cloud many times every day. To have access means you can use it.

DEVELOPMENT OF CLOUD STORAGE

The first computers were huge. They were called **mainframes**. Mainframes were very expensive. Companies paid to share computer time to save money. The idea of sharing computer resources led to the formation of the cloud. Resources are things that are used to do work.

Over time, computers got smaller. They also got more powerful. The first personal computers (PCs) were sold in the 1970s. Soon, PCs became more popular than mainframes. The amount of data their hard drives could store was very small. The amount grew over time.

PC users could save their data to external drives. Data can be words or images. "External" means outside the computer. External drives could

The first personal computers were sold in the 1970s.

Storing files is the most common use of cloud computing.

be flash drives or floppy disks. They were used to move files from one computer to another.

Early PC users could save their data to floppy disks like these.

Local storage had its problems. Some data became **corrupted** and it could not be accessed. External devices were also easily lost. Students might save homework on a floppy disk. They could not work on it at school if the disk was left at home. The cloud would make it easier to move and share data.

THINKING UP THE CLOUD

Joseph Carl Robnett Licklider (*left*) helped found cloud computing.

Joseph Carl Robnett Licklider is one of the founders of cloud computing. In 1962, he began writing about his idea for a computer network. His network would stretch across the world. He predicted many things that would happen with computers. In the 1960s, he created a network called the ARPANET. At first, it connected four university computers. The internet replaced ARPANET in the

1980s. ARPANET was shut down in 1990. Licklider died the same year, before the World Wide Web was started.

Computer scientist John McCarthy pictured the cloud in 1961. He imagined it as a public utility, like a phone or electric company. He thought users could pay to use as much data as they needed. People ignored McCarthy's idea when PC use became common. However, the cloud now is set up just as he saw it.

Flash drives can store more data than floppy disks.

The cloud solved another problem. Files were getting much bigger. Games and music could fill up all the storage on a PC. Storage is how much data a hard drive can hold. Videos were too big even for big PC hard drives. Cloud storage became the solution. Now, you don't have to store games on your computer. They are stored on the cloud. You can access them there through the internet.

Need for Speed

The first personal computers did not have internet access. The internet grew popular in the 1990s. At first, data moved over phone lines. It traveled slowly. People could not send big files. Today, we have high-speed internet. It can send a lot of information quickly. High-speed

Large files may cause computers to run out of local storage space.

internet made cloud storage possible. The cloud servers can be anywhere. Anyone with an internet connection can access the cloud. They

Many people today use tablets to access the cloud.

can use data stored anywhere in the world. They can get it quickly.

Now, many personal computers use clouds for most of their storage. This makes them

The internet makes cloud storage possible.

lighter and cheaper. Today, many more people can afford notebook computers and laptops. They can also use cloud apps on tablets and smartphones.

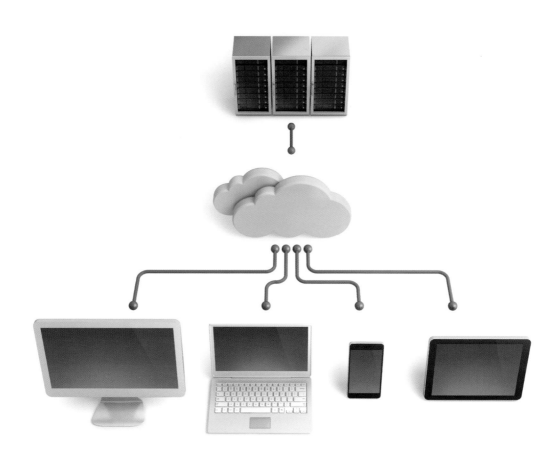

Servers control the flow of data on cloud networks.

CHAPTER 2
CLOUD TECHNOLOGY

The cloud is made up of many cloud networks. These networks operate programs. Some are available to the public. Everyone can use them. Some are owned by companies and are private. They are used only by people who work for that company. Some are **hybrids**. Hybrid clouds carry both public and private networks. They all work in the same way.

Local networks connect computers within the same business or location. Switches let these computers communicate. Routers link local networks and let them send data over the internet. Servers all over the world store and share this data.

A server is a computer that is bigger than a home computer. It runs faster. It can store and process much more information. A server has software that sends people data they ask for. It can send this information to any computer on the network. Every server on the cloud has its own job. The servers decide how information moves on the network.

ADVANTAGES OF THE CLOUD

Cloud technology has changed everyday life. Employers can store and access more data. Companies can share resources.

Cloud technology helps businesses grow.

This lets them spend less money on technology. They can also buy less software. Subscriptions to programs are often cheaper online than in stores. Businesses

Synchronization makes it easier for employees to work together.

can then spend money on other things that help them grow.

Sharing files allows people to work together more easily. They can exchange data instantly. For example, a doctor can look at medical records from another state. Two or more employees can edit files at the same time. This is called synchronization. Synchronization makes their information match.

Cloud users can work from home more easily. Companies save money on office space when employees work at home. Offices don't have to be as

Allowing employees to work from home can save businesses time and money.

big. Working from home also helps employees spend less time traveling to the office. It may let them work more flexible hours. It can decrease the need for expensive business trips.

The cloud has affected much more than the way we do business. Through apps such as Twitter and Instagram, it has changed the way we socialize. It allows students to take classes online. They can stream movies from their living rooms. Cloud-based companies have changed the way we shop. They've changed the way we find jobs. They have changed the way people find dates.

Concerns About the Cloud

Cloud users cannot retrieve files without internet access. This can be a problem. However, Wi-Fi lets you connect to the internet in many places, such as libraries and fast food restaurants.

Consumers spent $148 billion on cloud technology in 2016.

You can't connect to a flash drive that you left at home.

Security of data on the cloud can also be an issue. **Hackers** may steal online information. There may also be questions about who owns cloud data. If a company that stores data goes out of business, your files may disappear.

Encryption of data on the cloud makes it more secure. Encryption involves using codes so that hackers can't read the data. Developers

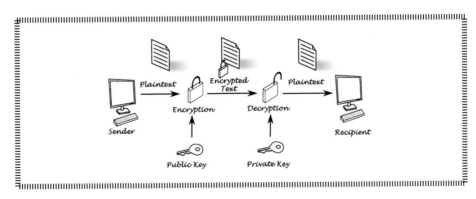

Encryption makes online data more secure.

Theft is common in restaurants. Some employees may take food without paying for it. They might give away free food to friends. They might add money to their own tips.

People often own more than one restaurant. They cannot be in two places at a time. That makes it hard for them to catch thieves in action. Security cameras used to be their only tool. They had to watch hours of video. They rarely had time. Now they have help from cloud software.

Theft is a common problem in restaurants.

CLOUD TECHNOLOGY IN ACTION

Cloud software looks at payment information from many restaurants. A program searches for suspicious patterns. It can find evidence of theft. This system saves owners time and money. It tells them what is going on in several restaurants at once.

Cloud software can help restaurant owners track payments and reduce their losses from theft.

There are many other ways businesses can save money using the cloud.

are trying to make online storage more safe and reliable.

THE FUTURE OF THE CLOUD

Cloud computing is expected to keep growing. Part of this growth may be in **artificial intelligence (AI)**.

Artificial intelligence trains computers to imitate human behavior. AI works by taking

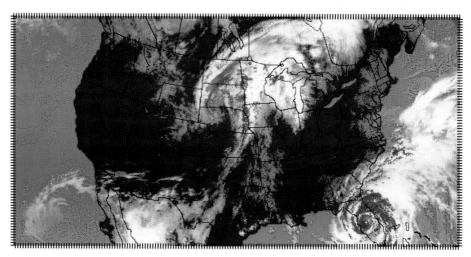
Artificial intelligence is used in weather forecasting.

The average company uses more than one thousand different cloud computing services.

in as much data as possible. A chess program plays so many matches that it "learns" every possible move.

AI can be used to catch hackers or to forecast weather. It can be used for virtual reality and entertainment.

Digital assistants collect answers to lots of questions. Cloud technology gives AI programs access to all those answers. It helps AI programs get smarter by giving them much more data. It lets businesses share expensive AI technology.

TECHNOLOGY TIMELINE

1944   IBM develops the first mainframe computer.

1962   Joseph Carl Robnett Licklider writes about his vision of a global computer network.

1981   IBM launches its first personal computer.

1991   The first web page goes live on the internet.

1997   The term "cloud computing" is first used by Professor Ramnath Chellappa.

1999   Salesforce provides a business model for cloud computing.

2006   Amazon Web Services and Google Docs are launched.

2011   IBM SmartCloud and iCloud are launched.

GLOSSARY

apps Computer programs made for certain tasks. They are often downloaded on smartphones or tablets.

artificial intelligence (AI) Computer technology set up to imitate human behavior.

bytes Units of computer memory.

corrupted Data that has been damaged or changed and made unusable.

data Information stored in and used by a computer.

hackers People who use computers to steal data.

hybrid Something that works using two types of systems.

local A computer or group of computers that is nearby.

mainframes Large computers that process huge amounts of data.

FIND OUT MORE

BOOKS

Smibert, Angie. *The Internet*. Burnsville, MN: Focus Readers, 2017.

Yomtov, Nel. *Internet Inventors*. New York: Scholastic, 2013.

WEBSITES

BBC Bitesize: How Does the Internet Work?

http://www.bbc.co.uk/guides/z3tbgk7

The Kid's Guide to How the Internet Works

http://www.attinternetservice.com/kids-internet-guide

INDEX

Jeanne Marie Ford is an Emmy-winning television scriptwriter and holds an MFA in writing for children from Vermont College. She has written numerous children's books and teaches college English. She lives in Maryland with her husband and two children.